CANADIAN NURSING SISTERS - THE FORGOTTEN HEROES.

William H. Graham

ISBN:

9 781777 125509

DEDICATION

I dedicate this book to the many Canadian Nursing Sisters who served their country valiantly.

In particular, I dedicate this book to the 12 nursing sisters who perished in the North Atlantic when the German Submarine sunk the Hospital Ship Llandovery Castle on June 27th., 1918.

I further dedicate this book to my Grand Aunt Elizabeth (Bessie) Fraser of New Glasgow who lost her daughter Margaret Marjorie Fraser on June 27th., her son Laurier Fraser killed three months earlier as well as her other son Alistair wounded twice, once at Vimy Ridge.

CONTENTS

CHAPTER 1

SOME HISTORY OF THE CANADIAN NURSING SISTERS

So often overlooked were the brave Canadian Nursing Sisters nicknamed the *"Bluebirds"* because of their white veils and blue dresses. These young women bravely volunteered for the First World War serving in tent hospitals, shacks on the front lines and on Hospital ships. Our troops referred to these sisters as **"angels of mercy"** while they saved the lives of those troops defending our democracy. In many cases they were almost at the front lines and in the same danger as the troops in order to help the wounded and get them additional help as quickly as possible.

But military nurses in Britain started back in 1854 with the Crimean War as the result of Florence Nightingale's campaign to convince the British government of the need for a medical corps. The British government did eventually agree and established this under a separate structure and in line with the suggestions of Florence Nightingale. During the Metis uprising in 1870 in Western Canada, Canadian volunteer nurses tended the injured soldiers at Red River. Later a larger group of nurses accompanied Canadian troops to Saskatchewan during the Northwest Rebellion. They became the medical and surgical department of the Canadian army. Eight nursing sisters tended wounded Canadian soldiers at Moose jaw and Saskatchewan field hospitals. Their work also had a significant impact on public attitudes, earning their occupation recognition as a legitimate profession for young women to aspire to and convincing the general public and politicians that they were more than capable to do this work.

When 1,000 Canadian soldiers went abroad for service in the Boer War (1899 – 1902) they were accompanied by four Canadian Nursing sisters who received pay and allowances and the rank of Lieutenant. Nurses were not accepted by the British unless they had a commission of at least Lieutenant.

Their numbers grew as an additional 5,000 soldiers volunteered for the South Africa conflict. At this point, in about 1904, it became obvious to the government and military leaders that the Canadian nurses were a necessary and most valuable part of the Canadian Army and nurses became part of the "reserves". Initially, 25 nurses were selected who would serve in times of need.

World War 1 saw many new nursing schools established across Canada and the nursing profession becoming more modern and popular to girls choosing a career.

The first CANC,s (Canadian Army Nursing Corps) Matron-in-Chief was Georgina Fane Hope. Nursing sister Georgina Hope served with distinction in both the Georgina Fane Pope was born January 1, 1862 in Prince Edward Island. The daughter of William Pope, a Father of the Confederation, she was a product of P.E.I gentility and could have doubtlessly had a comfortable marriage and became an island socialite. However, she instead travelled to New York, where she trained as a nurse at Bellevue Hospital.

In October 1899, after completing nursing studies at Bellevue Hospital in New York City, she volunteered for nursing service in the Second Boer War. Placed in command of the first group of nurses to go overseas, she served for more than a year in South Africa. For the first five months she and four other volunteer nurses served at British hospitals north of Cape Town. Next, Pope and another sister proceeded North to Kroonstadt where, despite shortages in food and medical supplies, took charge of a military hospital and successfully cared for 230 sufferers of fever.

In 1901, Pope, along with two other nurses, Deborah Hurcomb and Sarah Forbes, received medals for their war service from the Duke of York, later King George V, during his tour to the Outposts of the British Empire.

She returned there in 1902 as commander of the Canadian Army Nursing Service in charge of a second group of 8 Canadian nurses. She served at a hospital in Natal until the end of the war in May that year. In 1903, she became the first Canadian to receive the Royal Red Cross, awarded to her for meritorious and distinguished service in the field. She was also the first of 6419 females to receive this award.

In 1908 she was appointed first Matron of the Canadian Army Medical Corps.

In 1917, aged 55, Pope, although in poor health went to work near Ypres and served for the remainder of the Great War until 1918.

In April 1914, a few months before the start of WW 1, Margaret C. MacDonald was appointed the CANC's Matron-in –Chief. Margaret was from Bailey's Brook, in Pictou County, Nova Scotia.

Matron Margaret's experience dated back to the Boer war. Her experience helped her develop a model of how she felt the Canadian Army Nursing Corps should operate to be an effective service.

Note: *Letters I have from WW 1 nurses regard Matron Margaret MacDonald in high regard and nurses looked forward to her visits to their hospitals and casualty clearing stations.*

At the commencement of World War One, in August, 1914, there were only five Nursing Sisters in the Canadian military, with another 57 in reserve forces. By the end of the war they numbered over 2,000 with over 1,800 serving with overseas forces. These valiant ladies were referred to as "Nursing Sisters", although they were not affiliated with religious organizations. The role of these nursing sisters, as a result of their actions, changed their perception, and the perception of women in many ways.

During the first world war, Canadian nurses served valiantly in over thirty medical facilities in England, France, Galliipoli, Turkey, Alexandria, Egypt and Salonika, Greece.

Nursing sisters were deployed very near the front lines, temporarily at casualty clearing stations with doctors, where ambulances delivered the wounded to be assessed, treated or evacuated to a hospital. They worked under threat of daily death, capture, air raids and shell fire with an ever-changing battle front.

The workload was exhausting, and the conditions primitive and infections were common. Some nurses died after the war was over as a result of these diseases and infections. Despite their best efforts, equipment and medicines were scarce.

Patients requiring more care were moved to stationary hospitals close to the front lines. Each field hospital was organized so there was one matron supervising 16 nursing sisters. The hospital facilities were designed for 250 patients but generally handled more.

Those with serious injuries requiring longer hospital time were sent to general hospitals who could accommodate 500 or more beds. Nurses commonly were moved from one hospital to another as the needs changed.

Nurses and doctors had challenges they had not learned about in nursing or medical school, such as the horrific injuries from shells, poison gas, shrapnel and bullets.

The prolonged exposure to combat had resulted in many cases of soldiers suffering from Insomnia, night terrors, incontinence and shell shock. All thing not covered in the nurses training.

High mortality rates, as compared to their civilian nursing experiences, had a great effect on the nurses producing high stress levels resulting in fatigue and exhaustion. In many cases, nurses were hospitalized for short periods of time themselves to recover.

Nurses were often in the line of fire being close to the front and within range of the enemy guns for the benefit of the wounded. In one case in May 1918, in a field hospital near Etaples, and Doullens, France, enemy aircraft dropped bombs on five Canadian Stationary Hospitals, killing six Canadian nursing sisters.

Twenty-two Canadian nursing sisters also died of sickness or disease during these war years.

CHAPTER 2

WORLD WAR 1 - NEWS OF NURSES

London, Sept. 24. Six Canadian nurses were tonight gazetted as having won the military medal for bravery during enemy raids.

- **Matron Edith Campbell** of Point Claire attended wounded sisters regardless of personal danger;
- **Lenora Herrington** of Napanee, remained on duty the entire night and her personal example of courage was largely responsible for the maintenance of discipline and efficiency.
- **Lottie Urquhart ,** New Glasgow, N.S., when four bombs fell on her wards, attended the wounded with a courage and devotion which was an inspiring example.

- **Janet Mary Williamson** of Grenville, Quebec displayed exceptional coolness in a badly damaged ward, sustaining the patients and ensuring their evacuation.
- **Meta Hodge** of Hamilton and **Eleanor Jean Thompson** of Valleyfield, Quebec, although both injured by a falling beam, extinguished with great presence of mind, overturned oil stoves, later helping to remove the patients.

On March 3rd., 1916 The Toronto World published the following:

Nurses and Doctors were Inspected Yesterday and will Go Overseas to serve in a military hospital at Orpington, England.

The inspecting officer, Colonel Marlow, was pleased and described their appearance as fine with the 24 men in Khaki uniforms and the 81 women (nursing sisters) in trim uniforms. They were inspected in front of the parliament buildings.

The contingent had previously gathered in the railway committee's room in charge of Captains Munn and McLean. Here a few instructions were given, and then the word to fall in, two deep, in the corridor, from which the party marched to the inspection ground.

The girls in their smart new uniform of dark blue cloth with brass buttons, skirt, long coat with epaulets, soft felt hat and tan kid gloves, made a fine showing, their healthy complexions and good physique being noticeable.

Between the ranks marched the inspecting officer, the red band on his cap serving to mark his progress to the eyes of the spectators, of whom quite a number stood on the campus nearby.

The inspection over and Colonel Marlow evidently well pleased, the command was given and the party marched to the steps of the legislative building, where position was taken to be photographed by the numerous men with the cameras waiting the opportunity. The doctors in khaki centred the group, the nurses in their dark uniform forming a very attractive fringe.

The nurses for Orpington have been selected from all parts of Ontario, twenty of them because of their experience in hospitals for the insane, a psychiatric department being one of the specialities of the hospital to which they are going, as many men suffer from nervous diseases after the experiences of the trench or battlefield. Much credit is due S. A. Armstrong, assistant provincial secretary, for the expeditious and satisfactory military equipment of the unit, and to Dr. Helen MacMurchy, who had charge of the greater part of the organization and special training of the nurses.

CHAPTER 3

Canada in 1914 by the numbers

The CEF (Canadian Expeditionary Force) was comprised of men and women, some served only in Canada, but most serving overseas. The women in the CEF were almost exclusively in the Nursing Corps as Nursing Sisters with the rank of Lieutenant.

The population of Canada in 1914 was about 8 Million. 3.4 Million were males of Military age. Of that number, **617,000 males served in the CEF. 2,854 Females served in the CEF as Nursing Sisters**, mostly overseas. Some women in the CEF also served in other capacities such as cooking and laundry. Many Canadian nurses died in various ways including bombings and Gas. In one instances when the hospital was drenched with gas, the nursing sisters wore gas masks while they tended their patients. At one point a Colonel of one of the hospitals, having lost several nurses, decided to send them to a hospital closer to the coast and, at the time, immune to air raids. The nurses protested, declaring "We will carry on". The Colonel permitted them to remain.

CHAPTER 4

THE LETTER HOME

Nursing Sister Harriet Graham, from New Glasgow, NS, in a letter home on December 1914, gives the following description of a nurses typical duties at the first Canadian hospital the #2 Stationary Hospital in France.

"We have fifteen ambulances and they each carry four patients, and when they all make about three trips, it makes quite a number of patients." *"I'm not allowed to tell you how many patients we have or how many we can take, but you can tell Kit we can take twice as many as St. Luke's, and, of course, may have to take more than that at any time. Oh! My, but it is great. I just love it, even though it's ten o'clock now and I have been on the go all day, and they have not started to come in yet. I see where we don't get to bed tonight.*

By the time we get the poor souls into bed and half way clean and a dressing done, its morning before you know it, and the poor creatures, you would be sorry for them, they are so filthy, and many times just alive with vermin.

Pearl said tonight: "isn't it funny, in our hospital we despised men who were dirty, and here the worse they are, the better we like them." *When they say, "keep away sister, I'm so dirty, but I have been in the trenches, and I haven't had a bath for so many weeks,"* *I just feel like saying, "I honour your dirt-!"*

I hear we are getting a consignment of Germans tonight. I wonder sometimes if it is a sin to feel so awful for our enemies. I don't know if there is much in the papers at home about, them and the awful things they do."

Note: *The Pearl that Sister Harriet Fraser mentions is Marjorie Fraser, also of New Glasgow, NS, who lost her life in the Llandovery Castle sinking. They were 1ˢᵗ cousins.*

There were over 3,000 single women who served as nursing sisters in

Canadian Wounded Dressing Station in France - Oct. 1917

WWI. Their primary task was to provide comfort to the wounded and try to ensure a safe journey home on the hospital ships. In WWI, hospital ships were originally created and so nursing sisters would serve on them as well. As a result of their work, they were the first Canadian women to vote and considered to be just as important to the suffrage movement as Nellie McClung and the Famous Five.

53 nursing sisters lost their lives in the First World War. 14 of these brave sisters were drowned with the sinking of the one of the five Canadian hospital ships, the H.M.S. Llandovery Castle. These nursing sisters were all commissioned as Lieutenants in the Canadian Army Medical Corps.

CHAPTER 5

#2 STATIONARY HOSPITAL

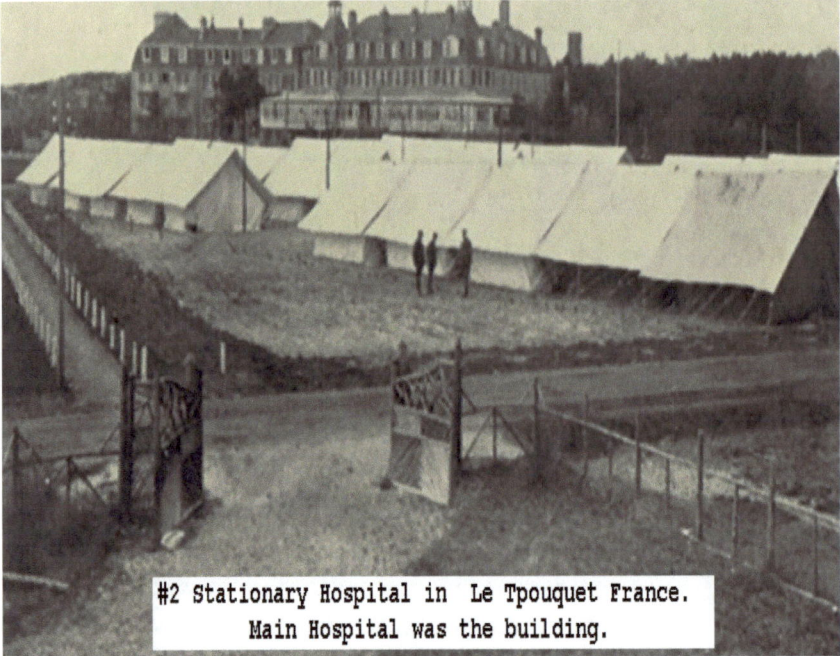

#2 Stationary Hospital in Le Tpouquet France.
Main Hospital was the building.

NOTE:

Harriet Graham of New Glasgow would have served at the #2 Stationary Hospital at Le Tqouquet, France. We see the building in the top of the picture and the verandas that they closed in to make the wards as described in Harriet's letter at the end of this text.

A correspondent of the **HUNTINGTON GLEANER** newspaper in Quebec gives his observations of the **No. 3 Canadian Hospital.** October 14th., 1915

A correspondent in France who visited the Canadian lines on his way back looked in to the hospitals, among them No. 3 of McGill University, of which Dr J.M. Elder is head surgeon. He writes:

Looking down from the ridge of sand hills, we saw between us and the English Channel a magnificent array of canvas tents. The hospital was McGill No. 3 General, and as we left our cars a little later on we were greeted by Colonel Birkett. At an early stage we peeped into the operating theater where we saw four patients under chloroform. One of them had a severe injury to the shoulder from shrapnel, and in the X-ray room we saw the photograph which indicated where the shrapnel had lodged. This operating theater had four chambers, in each of which operations could be carried on simultaneously.

The hospital is entirely under canvas, but huts will be provided for the nurses quarters before

CHAPTER 6

THE 14 BRAVE NURSING SISTERS

While many brave sisters gave their lives in wars, I will only deal with the 14 brave Canadian Nursing Sisters who drowned when the Llandovery Castle sank. The Llandovery Castle ship had been built in Glasgow and was named after a castle in Wales, but now she was a Canadian vessel. It was formerly a Union Castle Line Mail Steamship. Since the world had been plunged into the bloodiest war it had ever seen, the steamship had been turned into a floating hospital.

The Llandovery Castle , since March, 1918, had made four trips to Halifax, NS, returning thousands of wounded Canadian soldiers from the battlefields of Europe.. The hospital ship Llandovery Castle was sailing at a speed of about 14 knots and about 114 miles south-west of Faster Rock on the night of June 27th., 1918.

The ship had just brought 644 wounded soldiers home to Canada from the battlefields of Europe and was now on its return voyage to pick up more wounded patients, when it was torpedoed by a German U-Boat U-86.

As the Llandovery Castle churned across the North Atlantic, it was lit up by regulation Red Cross lights and markings, on the sides and top identifying it as a hospital ship.

According to international law, those markings should have offered it protection from patrolling German U-boats. They did not.

All hospital ships had lit Red Crosses on the sides and top signifying the ship was unarmed. The agreement was that enemy medical ships could be stopped and searched but not attacked.

The Llandovery Castle was Commanded by Capt. R.A. Sylvester a person considered to be an excellent seaman.

Despite this agreement, and with no warning, the commander of U-86, Helmut Brummer-Patzig fired a torpedo that struck the vessel "abaft" its No. 4 engines. A large portion of the ship was destroyed, disabling the engines with the captain losing all control. The initial blast also disabling the ships SOS system. Within ten minutes, the H.M.S. Llandovery Castle started to sink.

Effective evacuation procedures meant that all 258 passenger made it into the life boats before the ship sank. However a large section of the poop deck fell into the water creating a vortex (whirlpool). All nursing sisters were in one lifeboat and perished as the whirlpool tossed them into the sea consuming their lifeboat.

CHAPTER 7

SERGEANT KNIGHT'S DESCRIPTION

Sergeant Arthur Knight (Regimental number 528654) was one of the few survivors to describe the event. Sergeant Knight's skill and commitment was also credited with getting the lifeboats in the water so rapidly.

Sgt. Knight   Llandovery Castle

Sgt. Knight describes, in his words, the situation as follows:

"Unflinchingly and calmly, as steady and collected as if on parade, without a complaint or a single sign of emotion, our fourteen devoted nursing sisters faced the ordeal of almost certain death – only within a matter of minutes – as the lifeboat neared the mad whirlpool of water where all human power was helpless." "I estimate we were together in the boat about eight minutes. In the whole time I did not hear a complaint or murmur from one of the sisters.

There was not a cry for help or any evidence of fear. In the entire time I heard only one remark when the matron, Nursing Sister Margaret Fraser turned to me as we drifted helplessly towards the stern of the ship and asked: "Sergeant, do you think there is any hope for us?" "I replied, 'No,' seeing myself helpless without oars and the sinking condition of the stern of the ship. "

A few seconds later we were drawn into the whirlpool of the submerged afterdeck, and the last I saw of the nursing sisters was as they were thrown over the side of the boat. All were wearing life-belts, and of the fourteen two were in their nightdress, the others in uniform.

"It was,' concluded Sgt. Knight, "doubtful if any of them came to the surface again, although, I myself sank and came up three times, finally changing to a piece of wreckage and being eventually picked up by the captain's boat."

"For upwards of two hours the German submarine repeatedly attempted to blot out all traces of the crime by rushing to and fro among the wreckage and firing twenty or more shells from its large gun into the area where the life-boats were supposed to be afloat.

"That one boat survived is not the fault of the enemy, for at least three efforts were made to run it down, in addition to the shell fire directed towards it."

"After thirty-six hours afloat we were rescued by a torpedo-boat destroyer about fourty-one miles from the Irish coast, and taken to Queenstown, coming on to Plymouth, England on Sunday, June 30th, 1918."

At this point, Commander Helmut Brummer-Patzig and two other crew members of the U-86, Ludwig Dithmar and John Boldt, came on deck to interrogate the survivors. They demanded the location of "hidden ammunition" from the officers to which they truthfully said there was none. Not satisfied with this answer he ordered his crew to machine gun the survivors in the life boats.

One Nurse, Marjorie Fraser was asked to take tea back to France for the soldiers and refused because of their agreement not to carry anything but medical supplies. One life boat containing 24 people remained alive but adrift and probably out of the machine gunners range.

* The speculation is that when he realized that he had committed what amounted to a war crime, he ordered his men to destroy the evidence by ramming the remaining lifeboats and shooting the survivors.

They were picked up 36 hours later, after pulling on the oars for 70 miles, by the Canadian destroyer Lysander. The captain was landed at Queenstown.

CHAPTER 8

THE AFTERMATH

The sinking of the Llandovery Castle was the deadliest Canadian naval disaster of WWI. The manner in which the nursing sisters had lost their lives became quite well known, and was used as a rallying cry for Canadian troops during the battle of Amiens, one of the last great battles of the war.

Victory posters as we see on this cover page went up across Canada ant it served as a rallying point for men and women to enlist and for additional monetary and material support for the war during the last 100 day offensive.

The Victory Bond flyer clearly shows this. Indeed, that was effective, as the war ended that fall, Nov 11th, at 11 O'clock,1918.

Shamefully, Archival documents show that Canadian soldiers at Amiens were explicitly told that they would not be reprimanded if they killed German soldiers who had surrendered. It was tacit consent to enact a violent revenge for the deaths of the 14 nursing sisters.

Brig. –General George Tuxford gave instructions to his troops on August 8th., 1918 that the battle cry should be "Llandovery Castle," and "that cry should be the last to ring in the ears of the Hun as the bayonet was driven home."

Later, the captain of a British ship sailed through the wreckage. "Suddenly," he remembered, *"we began going through corpses.... we were sailing through floating bodies. We were not allowed to stop — we just had to go straight through."*

"It was quite horrific, and my reaction was to vomit over the edge. It was something we could never have imagined... particularly the nurses: seeing these bodies of women and nurses, floating in the ocean, having been there some time. Huge aprons and skirts in billows, which looked almost like sails because they dried in the hot sun."

Dithmar and Boldt were presented at the Leipzig Trials, receiving sentences of four years hard labour but escaped on route to prison.

The commander of U-86, Helmut Brummer-Patzig disappeared without a trace without being brought to justice for this horrendous crime.

However when Hitler launched a Second World War, there was a familiar face on his payroll. Captain Patzig had been welcomed back into the German navy. And this time, he was in charge of an entire flotilla, training a new generation of German submariners how to wage war. He lived to the age of 93 yrs.

CHAPTER 9

THE ADMIRALTY STATEMENT

Some slight differences

"It was during the night of June 27th, towards 10:30 that the crime occurred. The Llandovery Castle steaming on her course at some 14 Knots showed the usual navigation and Hospital ship lights. Under the overcast sky she was plain to see and could not be mistaken for any but what she was - a ship immune by every law of war and peace from attack or molestation.

All lights were burning when the ship was torpedoed. These included a large electric cross over the bridge and strings of white and green lights on either side. ***The Red crosses on the sides of the Vessel were illuminated by electric lights.***

"No one on board saw the wake of the torpedo. The first intimation of the presence of a submarine was a jar and the roar of an explosion from aft. Then the lights went out. All that followed, save when a dim light obtained from the emergency Dynamo just before the ship floundered. The engines were running to stop then full speed astern, but from the engine room came no answer." With no one to shut off the power, the ship continued moving until the engine room flooded and shut off the power. In the Wireless cabin the Marconi operator tried in vain to transmit the ship's position. His key gave no response, the spark was gone.

The carpenters report was that the number four hold aft was blown and the ship could not remain afloat.

Except for the engine room hands, all 258 people were able to get into life boats within the ten minutes it took for the ship to sink.

The U-boat captain then brought his submarine to the surface and began shelling the life boats. Five of the life boats were never seen again. The boat in which Margaret was in, was overturned by the wash of the submarine and Margaret was one of those drowned. There were less than 30 survivors.

The Admiralty reported that after the sinking the submarine shelled an unknown target that might have been the missing life boats.

The Submarine hailed the ship to come alongside. He made the Captain come aboard the submarine and argued that they were carrying American Flight Officers. The Captain was let go and he got in the small boat. He could see nothing of the others. With no wireless being sent out there was no hope for assistance. The Captain decided to head for the Irish coast and after sailing and pulling on the oars for about 70 miles he was picked up by a destroyer which immediately sent out a distress signal to look for survivors . They landed the Captain at Queenstown."

End of Admiralty report:

CHAPTER 10

SUSPICION – DENIAL - OUTRAGE

THE FIRST SUSPICION: The sinking of the hospital ship Llandovery Castle, with its evidence of her sailing having been betrayed by a spy, has roused resentment to such a degree in England that there is an insistent demand that all Germans be interned and their families sent back whence they came. In the discussion in Parliament Premier George agreed drastic action was called for, and added. It was difficult to preserve one's temper when one heard of aliens crowing about German victories.

There was never a case of a British setback when he did not get numerous letters written by Germans in Britain crowing over it. These letters bore a British postmark, and obviously were written by Germans. That sort of thing must be stopped. The American people desire like legislation. Evidence that millions have been subscribed by wealthy residents of German origin to stir up opposition to the government and to destroy factories and storehouses has evoked a bitter feeling.

The strikes which are hindering the shipment of troops and supplies to France are blamed upon them. In fact, wherever in the States or Canada disaffection is found, Germans fan it by their agents.

The world was outraged by the sinking of the Hospital Ship Llandovery Castle as these newspaper articles indicate..

This is a series of articles condeming the sinking of the Canadian Hospital Ship Llandovery Castle

BERLIN   DENIAL   - London Times   - July 4, 1918 -
LLANDOVERY CASTLE

Amsterdam, July 2. Without waiting for the supplementary intelligence which has proved that a German submarine sank the. Llandovery Castle, Berlin, with imprudent haste, has issued the following semi-official communiqué:-

Like all similar assertions of the British Admiralty it is probably (duerfie) in this case also incorrect that a German U-boat is responsible for the ship's fate. It appears from later news that no one on board the steamer observed a U-boat or a torpedo. At all events the cause of the loss may be attributed to a -British mine.

July 3.—It would appear from a Berlin official semi-official dispatch issued this morning by the Wolff Bureau that the German, authorities have not allowed the full statement regarding the sinking of the Llandovery Castle to be printed in Germany. Otherwise, the dispatch in question, which is quoted below, is scarcely intelligible:

First it is said that the Llandovery Castle was clearly recognizable as a hospital ship, although all proof is lacking for this assertion. Secondly how could the submarine commander know that Canadian airman were on board? Thirdly, the Canadian Government, as is alleged, chartered the vessel also for prisoners, but assert nevertheless that they have not transported any prisoners of war in the vessel during the last six months. Fourthly, the assertion that the German U-boat fired at the boats is without doubt a barefaced untruth. Fifthly, the report of the submarine commander on the events accompanying the sinking of the ship must be awaited.

U.S. VIEWS ON "THE UNSPEAKABLE PRUSSIAN" (FROM OUR CORRESPONDENT) NEW YORK, July 3. Since the sinking of the Lusitania no German crime has affected the American nation quite so deeply as the torpedoing of the Llandovery Castle. It was with peculiar grimness that the nation turned to-day from studying details of this latest exploit in fiendishness to the announcement of President Wilson that over 1,000,000 troops are in France and to statistics of the Shipping Board showing the phenomenal growth of American sea tonnage.

America feels that it has the resources and the will, together with the Allies, finally to overcome the bestial horror which infests the seas and ravages the land in the name of the German Emperor.

"The Unspeakable Prussian" is the title under which the cartoonist to-day interprets the event, while editorial writers are concerned mainly with schemes for a long excommunication of the German people from intercourse with the civilized world.

The *New York Times* says:

The Hague Convention gives belligerents the right to visit hospital ships. But these cold-blooded assassins refused to exercise that right; they strike and slay because it is in their hearts to glut their cruelty upon helpless non-combatants after trumping up a case of justification, which is only another infamy. The Allies in presence of this crowning atrocity have a duty to perform. A German officer recently captured said, "We are going to win, or we are going to hell." The Germans are not going to win, but if there is hell for Germans in retribution, the Parliaments and Legislatures of the Allies should ensure that retribution.

The British Seamen's Union has blazed the way, and it is for the statesmen of Allied countries to formulate and sanction the plan. To talk of reprisals is vain. Punishment should take the form of excommunication, isolation, and deprivation, until the guilty nation makes amends and qualifies for re-admission to civilization.

CONDEMNATION IN HOLLAND (FROM OUR SPECIAL CORRESPONDENT)

THE HAGUE, July 2. The sinking of the Llandovery Castle has caused more indignation here than any incident connected with the war of recent date. The newspapers comment in severe terms, and even the Vaderland, which, to put it mildly, certainly cannot be accused of anti-German sympathies, speaks out ' with no uncertain voice. The journal says: The assertion that a few American flight officers were making use of the hospital ship is also singular, because approximately 1,000,000 American troops, thanks to their admirably organized transport service, have been conveyed safe and sound to France, showing that flight officers can safely proceed to their destination without the misuse of hospital ships.

Yet this suspicion seems to have given the occasion to the German submarine commander to torpedo the Llandovery Castle without warning. This is an important point. Submarines are destroyed by dozens by artfully laid submarine traps, and where the German Admiralty desires to spare its submarines it has resorted to the destruction of every vessel within a dangerous region without investigation or warning. So long, however, as it is unproved that a hospital ship is ever employed as a submarine trap, no reason exists to employ this reckless method against it also.

The suspicion of conveying munitions and sound troops existed - whether rightly or wrongly we do not discuss; we merely point out that the suspicion has never been supported on sufficient grounds. But such suspicions are insufficient to sink a hospital ship proceeding with full lights and marks, without warning or search. It must be proved that hospital ships are misused as submarine traps.   .
But no such proof has appeared.

According to The Hague Convention, the submarine commander had full right to detain and search the Llandovery Castle. His reckless action will therefore rightly arouse the greatest indignation not of the enemy alone but also of neutrals ... Fairness demands that we should await the defense of the other side, but we cannot imagine that it can do away with the grave accusation which the occurrence involves.

CANADIAN MEDICAL STAFF (FROM OUR OWN CORRESPONDENT) - TORONTO, July 2.

There is much feeling throughout Canada over the sinking of the Llandovery Castle. The vessel made many trips to and from Halifax, and brought back thousands of wounded soldiers. Among the medical staff were Major MacDonald and his brother, Dr. H.C. MacDonald, of Halifax, while the matron was Margaret Marjoric Fraser, of New Glasgow, Nova Scotia and Saskatoon, youngest daughter of Mr. D. C. Fraser, formerly Liberal member of Parliament, afterwards a Judge, and at his death lieutenant-Governor of Nova Scotia.

On board also was Nursing Sister Gallaher, of Ottawa, formerly superintendent of Moose Jaw Hospital. As yet the newspapers are unable to secure full lists of the Canadian doctors and nurses.

FROM THE PSALMIST. - TO THE EDITOR OF THE TIMES.

Sir, Immediately after reading the story in The Times this morning of the last German horror it was my duty, being a schoolmaster, to go to morning chapel. The Psalm for the day seemed strangely and terribly appropriate. It was Psalm xi.

I need only quote the second and third verses as they are given in the 'Revised Version:

• For, lo, the wicked bend the bow,
They make ready their arrows upon the string,
That they may shoot in darkness at the upright of heart.
If the foundations be destroyed,
What can the righteous do?

The Psalmist gives the answer, the only answer that can be given, in the verses that follow. I think that many readers may be glad to have their attention drawn to this example of one instance of what Dean Church calls "those piercing, lightning-like gleams of strange spiritual truth" contained in the Psalms.

July 2. Yours faithfully, U.

LONDON TIMES - LLANDOVERY CASTLE OUTRAGE.: NO MORE SURVIVORS.

BERLIN PREPARING EXCUSES.

The Secretary of the Admiralty makes the following announcement:

The area between the spot where the Llandovery Castle was sunk by a German submarine on Thursday last and the South-West Irish Coast has now been thoroughly searched by two groups of H.M. ships, in addition to H.M.S. Lysander, and only a little wreckage and one empty boat has been found. It may, therefore, be assumed that there are no more survivors from the Llandovery Castle.

Amsterdam, July 2.—Berlin is already preparing the way for German excuses regarding the torpedoing of the Llandovery Castle. While making no specific reference to this disaster, the semi-official German agency has telegraphed abroad a quotation from the Madrid newspaper Correspondencia Militar, as published in the Cologne Gazette, maintaining, despite the Spanish Foreign Minister's declarations to the contrary, that the British authorities continue to make improper use of the Red Cross flag.—Reuter.

INDIGNATION IN AMERICA. - (FROM OUR OWN CORRESPONDENT.)

WASHINGTON, JULY 1. Not since Germany's declaration of ruthless submarine warfare, which forced the United States into the war, has Washington been swept with such a wave of horror and indignation as by the sinking of the hospital ship Llandovery Castle by a German submarine. The Americans, however, are not surprised at this new outrage, but the German charges that American airmen are conveyed in hospital ships in order to ensure their safe arrival arouses the bitterest resentment. When a German newspaper suggested that the American hospital ship Comfort, which was sent to France without a naval convoy, might transport American airmen, Mr. Lansing declared that Germany was seeking to justify- herself in advance for any outrage that might be committed against the hospital ships of the Allies. The feeling hero is that his prophecy has been eloquently borne out by this latest crime.

DUTCH VIEW OF THE CRIME. - (FROM OUR SPECIAL CORRESPONDENT.)

THE HAGUE, JULY 2. The Handelsblad, commenting on the sinking of the Llandovery Castle, says :-

Again a hospital ship has been torpedoed, again a repulsive crime has been committed, which- is not only against international law, but a deed which arouses horror because it conflicts with every idea of humanity.

Is this intentional? Were orders given by authority to torpedo, in contravention of every convention, ships which bear clear signs that they are manned according to the Geneva Convention, which was recognized by all the Powers? Is the story that hospital ships are used for the transport of ammunition or troops so generally accepted that every hospital ship is already doomed in advance?

Or is it an act of a submarine commander become unaccountable in his actions through war, and through his inhuman work? The first appears to be the case. Thinking that American flight officers were on board the Llandovery Castle, the submarine commander, without closer investigation, without ascertaining the accuracy of his opinion, sank the hospital ship.

There is no excuse for such a deed. The shocking nature of such actions on the part. of submarine commanders has frequently been pointed out, and frequently severely condemned - and yet they continue, with their

Government's approval, or at any rate without anything being said against it from the German side in the shape of an open disavowal of their unholy action.

In his latest speech, Herr von Kuhlmann spoke of the spirit of distrust at present existing and rendering all rapprochement impossible. He hoped-that soon a certain degree of confidence in each other's chivalry and decency might be restored. How is that possible with such un-chivalrous and scandalous deeds, with the betrayal of every idea of loyalty to humanity, to say nothing of the violation of treaties concluded and signed? To expect this chivalry and decency from the opposite party, but to tread it under foot oneself, is not the way to realize

Herr von Kuhlmann's wish. The beginning of improvement is to contribute to it oneself by condemning un-chivalrous deeds and by openly expressing indignation at them. To defend murder, to order or to approve of a brutal attack on non-combatants is as worthy of condemnation as to commit murder - unless, indeed, there be two moralities, one for individual and one for political use.

FIVE YEARS' MORE BOYCOTT. - July 3, 2018 Mr. Havelock Wilson, president of the National Sailors and Firemen's Union, yesterday received a telegram from Mr. C. McVey, the district secretary of the union at Liverpool, stating that at a meeting of 600 seamen and stewards held at Liverpool yesterday the fallowing resolution was adopted

"That this meeting of Liverpool seamen and stewards strongly protest against the latest crime of the Huns in sinking the Llandovery Castle hospital ship without warning, and we hereby request Mr. Havelock Wilson to add another five years to the boycott of Germany fur this most diabolical and cowardly murder of our brothers on the sea."

Mr. Bonner Law, in his speech at the meeting of the Inter-Parliamentary Commercial Conference at the House of Lords yesterday referred to the outrage. The action of the Germans was, he said, contrary even to the principles which they now professed.

CHAPTER 11

BURIAL INFORMATION – THE HALIFAX MEMORIAL

The **HALIFAX MEMORIAL** in Nova Scotia's capital, erected in Point Pleasant Park, is one of the reminders of the men and women who died at sea including these 14 brave nurses. Twenty-four ships were lost by the Royal Canadian Navy in the Second World War and nearly 2,000 members of the RCN lost their lives. This Memorial was erected by the Commonwealth War Graves Commission. The monument is a great granite Cross of Sacrifice over 12 metres high, visible to all ships approaching Halifax. The cross is mounted on a large podium bearing 23 bronze panels upon which are inscribed the names of over 3,000 Canadian men and women who were buried at sea.

Most of these nursing sisters are additionally remembered in memorials in their respective towns or cities across Canada.

The dedicatory inscription, in French and English, reads as follows:

1914-1939   -   1918-1945

**IN THE HONOUR OF
THE MEN AND WOMEN OF THE NAVY
ARMY AND MERCHANT NAVY
OF CANADA
WHOSE NAMES**

**ARE INSCRIBED HERE
THEIR GRAVES ARE UNKNOWN
BUT THEIR MEMORY**

SHALL ENDURE.

On June 19, 2003, the Government of Canada designated *September 3rd*. of each year as a day to acknowledge the contribution of Merchant Navy Veterans.

The following pages will describe the 14 brave Canadian nursing sisters who died on June 27th., 1918 with the sinking of the Llandovery Castle Hospital Ship

Nursing Sisters:

- Carola Josephine Douglas, Toronto, ON
- Alexina Dussault, St. Hyacinthe, QB
- Minnie Aenath Follette, Port Greville, NS
- Margaret Jane Fortescue, York Factory, MN
- Matron Margaret Marjory 'Pearl' Fraser, New Glasgow, NS / Moose Jaw SK
- Minnie Katherine Gallaher, Kingston, ON
- Jessie Mabel McDiarmid, Ashton, ON
- Mary Agnes McKenzie, Toronto, ON (Plaque in Calvin Presbyterian Church, Toronto)
- Christina Campbell, Victoria, BC (Plaque in Royal Jubliee Hospital)
- Rena 'Bird' McLean, Souris, P.E.I. (Exhibit and memorial in Souris)
- Mary Belle Sampson, Simcoe, ON (Plaque in Hamilton, ON)
- Gladys Irene Sare, Montreal QB (Plaque in Montreal General Hospital)
- Anna Irene Stamers, St. John, NB
- Jean Templeman, Ottawa, ON

Officers who lost their lives on the Llandovery Castle

Lieutenant Colonel Thomas Howard Macdonald – PH, CB

Major Gustavus Mitchell Davis

Captain William James Enright

Captain Arthur Vincent Leonard

Captain George Luther Sills

Honourary Captain Donald George MacPhail (Rev.)

Honourary Captain and **Chaplain Donald George MacPhail**

Son of Donald and Christina MacPhail, of Perth, Ontario. Husband of Louisa B. MacPhail, of 35, King St. West, Kingston, Ontario.

Rev. Donald George MacPhail

Enlisted Men

536451 Private John Anderson

421053 Private Hubert Tyndall Angus

536234 Private Albert Baker

33281 Private Frank Barker

2568 Private John Arthur Bentley

50972 Lance Corporal Hugh Bonnell

524507 Private James Frederick William Bristow

2098951 Sergeant Daniel Brown

526511 Private Neville Raymond Stevenson Carter

962 Private William Frederick Cates

536231 Private Frederick Clark

536448 Private William Clark

536023 Private Walter Cowie

526671 Private John Henry Curtis

536282 Private Kenneth Daley

823269 Lance Corporal William Albert Dawson

536338 Private David William Duffie

418883 Private Alexander Livingstone Dunlop

50379 Private John Eaton

523837 Private Harley Clifton Elsley

34408 Staff Sergeant Herbert Harold Evans

645609 Private Robert Douglas Falconer

50946 Private James Benedict Foley

522922 Private Wilfred Howie Gemmel

535505 Private Myer Philip Goldberg

770053 Private James Hannah

33354 Private Matthew Henry Harlock

33079 Private Bertram Harris

536276 Private Harry Harrison

524248 Private George Edward Harvey

40310 Private Clifford Hugh Hoskins

T/815 Private Sidney Isaac

33653 Corporal William Jackson
535449 Private Wilfred Lawrence James
195880 Private Robert Carman Kelly
536277 Private Edward Moore Macpherson
27150 Private Frederick Leo McAnally
526600 Private James Henry Murray McDermott
2098858 Private Leonard Hugh McDonald
525169 Private John McGarry
644511 Private George Edward Nash
213383 Private Norman Robert O'Neil
467562 Private John Cooper Pateman
81693 Private Herbert Arthur Patton
1390 Private Frederick Pollard
525545 Private John Porter
50089 Private John Arthur Purcell
524579 Private Alfred Renyard
523324 Private Percy Richards
910940 Private Kelby Roseboro
536477 Private Walter Bramwell Sacre
644708 Private Victor Sanders
527999 Private Walter Harry Sanders
536403 Private Robert Andrew Sanderson
862726 Private Frederick Jacob Sayyae
536249 Private Clement George Scribner
524307 Private Lewis Shipman
527654 Private Ernest Crosby Smith
3676 Private David Radcliffe Smuck
536315 Private John Spittal
400171 Private Robert Alexander Steen
536236 Private Frank Chandler Williams
530063 Private Robert Williams
527674 Private Andrew Wilson

Nursing Sister Christina Campbell
1877-1918

Christina was born on August 17th., 1877 in Beauly, Invernesshire, Scotland to Alexander and Harriet MacDonald of Victoria, British Columbia. Her parents were born and married at Glen Morrison of Urquhart in Scotland.

Nursing Sister Christina Campbell

Christina had one brother, Angus Campbell, who was living in Victoria, B.C. Christina was a graduate of the Royal Jubilee Hospital School of Nursing in Victoria, British Columbia, graduating in the class of 1897, with about 45 other Nursing Sisters.

In 1915 Christina went to London, Ontario and on September 15th., 1915, Christina enlisted in the Canadian Army Medical Corps. Her will stated that all her personal effects were to go to her brother Angus. After six weeks of training at the Halifax Infirmary Hospital in Nova Scotia, Christina received her first post to #2 Canadian General Hospital in France. The hospital had only been open for six months and was a tent hospital holding just over 1,000 beds.

The work was gruelling with Sisters having to cope with lack of vital medicines, pests like rats and fleas and the inhumane work hours.

In mid-November of 1915, Christina transferred to #5 CGH in London, England where she worked as part of the Medical Evacuation Force, ferrying wounded soldiers to various hospitals in England. During the following year, Christina worked at a tent hospital in Egypt and a new hospital in Salonica, Malta.

The five months in Salonica, Malta were punishing with two months of continuous night duty resulting in her developing insomnia and a depression-like mental illness called Neurasthenia.

Other sisters noticed Christina losing weight, not sleeping at night and completing all her rounds with tears streaming down her face.

The continual night shift, extreme heat, isolation and horrific scenes Christina worked with daily destroyed her mental state. Christina was given leave to recover in England at the Kings Cross Canadian Red Cross Convalescent Hospital.

After a few months in England regaining her strength, Christina returned to the #5 CGH medical evacuation force.

In August she began work at the Eye and Ear Hospital in Westcliffe staying until March 1918, when Christine was posted to the H.M.S Llandovery Castle Hospital ship.

The story of the sinking of the Llandovery Castle on its voyage from Halifax back to England has already been told on previous pages.

Christina's medals included (1914-15 Star, British War medal, Victory medal) and Memorial Plaque and Scroll sent to her brother Angus Campbell 1008-1010 Government street Victoria, British Columbia

Christina's grave reference is found on Panel 2 of the Halifax Memorial.

Nursing Sister Carola Josephine Douglas 1874 – 1918

Carola Josephine Douglas was born in 1874 in Costa Rica. Carola also had a brother Arthur, born in 1877.Carola's parents were Captain Andrew Trew Douglas and his wife Juanita Douglas. Captain Andrew was eight years old when he and his eight siblings emigrated from Ireland. He was an Engineer and sea captain on the Great Lakes and led an adventurous life sailing the oceans of South America. In Panama he met his wife Jaunita Lanus (Lasas), a beautiful lady of Spanish descent.

Captain Andrew used his engineering skills working for many groups including one French group attempting to build the Panama Canal. His adventures took them to engineering projects in Costa Rica and there Carola Josephine was born in 1874, followed by a brother, Arthur in 1877.

In May 1884, Captain Andrew, Juanita and the children travelled from Panama to New York…A few days after their arrival, Andrew became gravely ill and died. Within a couple of days, Juanita also died leaving their children orphans. Family members in Toronto and Winnipeg took the children in and census records became confused and they were listed as Canadian born.

Carolas' nursing career began at the Pennsylvania Hospital in Philadelphia. Carola was a great traveller, living in New York, but visiting Bermuda, Panama, Scotland, England and Yugoslavia.

Carolas' photo still hangs in the halls of Harbord Collegiate as part of their war memorial and a memorial to all their former students who died during the war stands outside the school.

In 1915, Carolas' trip to Australia was cut short when she heard that war had broken out in Europe. She returned home to her sister's home in Winnipeg and there she enlisted in the Canadian Army Medical Corps.

On February 18th., 1915 Nursing sister Carola arrived at Liverpool, England aboard the S.S. Zeeland along with many brave women of the first contingent of the C.A.M.C. Netheravon House in Wiltshire, U.K. was Carola's first destination.

Netheravon House was a convalescent home for wounded Canadian troops, and it was here that Nursing sister Carola'a attestation papers were signed on March 4th., 1915.

After a period in England, Nursing Sister Douglas did a tour in France, later to Saloniki then after several months in the Balkan war theatre, she was posted to the Llandovery castle Hospital ship. Nursing Sister Coralo also died with the sinking of the Llandovery Castle. This had been her third voyage.

The story of the sinking of the Llandovery Castle on its voyage from Halifax back to England has already been told on previous pages.

Nursing Sister Carola's medals included British War medal, Victory medal) at least.

Nursing Sister Carola Josephine Douglas grave reference is found on

Panel 2 of the Halifax Memorial.

Nursing Sister Alexina Dussault
1882 – 1918

Nursing Sister Alexina Dussault was born on March 25, 1882 in Saint-Hyacinthe, Quebec.

She was the daughter of Napoleon Dussault and Octavie Laliberte.

Alexina Dussault (1875-1918) was born, according to her attestation papers, in Saint-Hyacinthe, Quebec, in 1882. It is possible that she claimed to be younger than she was in order to be allowed to enlist.

Alexia Dussault was one of the 120 graduates of the Royal Victoria Hospital nursing program who served overseas.

I believe a picture of her hangs in the hospital.

A. Dussault, drowned by the torpedoeing of the Llandovery Castle.
27. vi. 18.

IWM

Sister Dussault studied to become a nurse, and it is in this role that she joined the Canadian Expeditionary Force on September 25, 1914, at Quebec City. She would have been a recipient of the Mons Star as she was in the first Canadian contingent.

In 1901 census records list Alexinas' age as 26 and living with her parents in the St. Antoine Ward of Montreal at 673 Cadieux St. Her father was a machinest. Nursing Sister Dussault was immediately assigned to the Nursing Service of the Canadian Army Medical Corps

(C.A.M.C.), later on August 1916 she was posted to the No. 1 Canadian General Hospital, and then to the No. 2 Canadian Stationary Hospital.

The following May she was transferred to 16th Canadian General Hospital in Orpington, England.

Like the majority of military nurses, Sister Dussault treated sick and wounded soldiers in auxiliary and field hospitals in Europe.

After 35 days' leave in Canada, she joined the HMHS LETITIA, a hospital ship.

In February 1916, records show that she was working "in the field" in Boulogne, France.

Nurses were also needed, however, to care for soldiers being sent back to Canada on hospital ships.

In July to December 1917 – She is posted to the King's Canadian Red Cross Convalescent Hospital in Bushy Park, England, and then to the hospital ship ARAGUAYA. In November she is attached again to King's Cross Hospital,

Nursing Sister Dussault volunteered for this duty, and during her service made many trips between England and Canada.

On March 25, 1918   Sister Dussault was posted to the HMHS LLANDOVERY CASTLE

However on June 27, 1918, she was on the hospital ship LLANDOVERY CASTLE as it sailed from Halifax, Nova Scotia, to Liverpool, England, when it was torpedoed by a German U-boat and sunk, taking her to her death with her fellow nurses.

Nursing Sister Alexina Dussault's medals included The Mons Star, British War medal, Victory medal) at least.

Nursing Sister Alexina Dussault grave reference is found on

Panel 2 of the Halifax Memorial.

Mons Star	British War Medal	WW I Victory Medal

All those serving in the first World War would receive the British War Medal and the WW 1 Victory Medal.

Those who were in the first contingent going overseas between August and November, 1914 also received the Mons Star.

Others received additional medals for others things they accomplished.

Nursing Sister Minnie Asenath Follette
1884 - 1918

Nursing Sister Minnie Follette was born on Nov 11th., 1884 at Port Greville, Nova Scotia.

She was a daughter of Oscar Adelbert Follette and Lydia Follett of Cumberland County, Nova Scotia.

Her sister was Beatrice Emily Edna Wilson and brothers, John Follette and Joseph Ashford Follette.

She enlisted in the Nursing Sister Army Corps (Permanent Forces) on November 11th, 1911.

Sister Folette enlisted on September 24th., 1914 as one of the first nurses to enlist in the Canadian Expeditionary Force (CEF) and Canadian Army Medical Corps (CAMC).

Sister Follette was stationed with the 1st Canadian Casualty Station.

M.A. Follette, drowned by the torpedoeing of H.M Hospital Ship Llandovery Castle June 27 1918.

From there she went with the Medical Corps Orpington.

Sister Follette was diagnosed with a nervous exhaustion on April 8th, **1916**. She got two months of rest.

Nursing Sister Minnie Follette was hospitalised at the 3rd Canadian General Hospital from bronchitis from March 22nd to April 6th, **1917**.

Posted on the HMS Letitia on August 2nd., 1917

Posted at the Ontario Military Hospital on October 5th., 1917

Posted on the Llandovery Castle (Hospital ship) March 22nd, **1918**.

She drowned in the sinking of the Llandovery Castle on June 27th at the age of 33 with thirteen other Nursing Sisters.

Her medals (1914-15 Star, British War Medal, Victory Medal), Memorial Plaque and Scroll were sent to her father Oscar A. Follette.

Her Memorial Cross was sent to her mother Lydia Follette. Nursing Sister Minnie Asenath Follette grave reference is found on Panel 2 of the Halifax Memorial.

Nursing Sister Minnie Asenath Follettes' grave reference is found on

Panel 2 of the Halifax Memorial.

AGE OF NURSES

I have found differences between the ages of several nurses on their enlistment documents and the census documents. Because of age restrictions, some nurses reduced their age 6 or 8 years.

Sister Margaret Jane Fortescue
1878 - 1918

Sister Fortescue was born in 1878 in Keewatin, Canada. At a young age she was sent home to Dawlish, to Miss Suzan Parrott's Ladies' School for her education. She was the ward of her aunts while here. She then returned to Canada where she was trained as a nurse.

Sister Fortescue was one of 12 children;

Matthew (1866-) ,

Annie Maud Marie (1867-),

Caroline Elizabeth (1869-1871),

Hugh (1870-1870) (infant death) , Frances Eleanor (1871- 1928),

Gertrude Edith May (1873-)

Charles Le Geyt (1878- 1936),

Margaret Jane (1878-1918),

John Percival (1879),

twins George Godfrey (1886- 1916),

Joseph Edward Barrington (1886-1898)

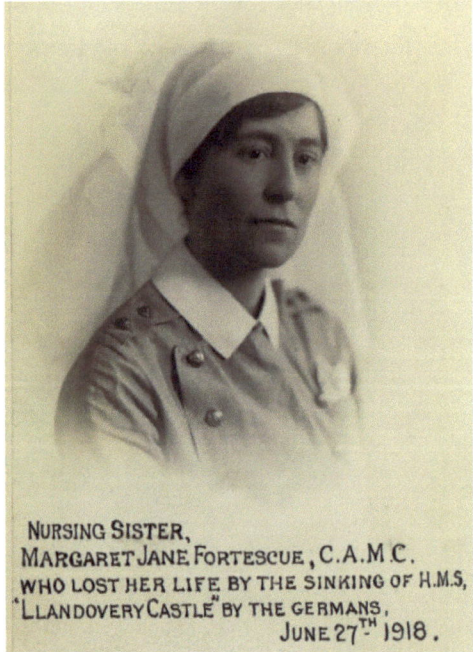

NURSING SISTER, MARGARET JANE FORTESCUE , C.A.M.C. WHO LOST HER LIFE BY THE SINKING OF H.M.S. "LLANDOVERY CASTLE" BY THE GERMANS, JUNE 27TH 1918 .

Sister Fortescue was the daughter of Joseph Fortescue, Chief Factor of the   Hudsons Bay Company and his wife, Sarah Jane. They were married at York Factory, Northwest Territories, Canada on 14 September, 1864.

Sarah Jane (Sister Fortescues' mother) was daughter of the Rev. Mason, D.D., of Northumberland and a granddaughter of the Matthew Fortescue, County Court Judge, of Totnes, Devon.

Sister Fortescue was trained as a Nurse at the Montreal General Hospital.

She volunteered for foreign service, and joined the Canadian Red Cross In 1915. Sister Fortescue served with the Expeditionary Force in France and Flanders from 18 May, 1915, being posted to various hospitals and casualty clearing stations there.

She was posted to H.M. Hospital Ship Llandovery Castle on the 5th. of June, 1918, and was lost when that ship was torpedoed and sunk in the Irish Sea on the 27th of the same month.

The Director of Medical Service, in London, wrote: ". . . Sister Fortescue was untiring in her efforts to do everything humanly possible for the sick and wounded under her care," "As a former patient, a private in the Canadian Army; **"The Little Mother"** (the name bestowed upon her by the patients whom she nursed) has earned the V.C. as much as any man in the Army.

…….. .. Four years of untiring labour and fearless devotion, often caring for the wounded and the dying with the sound of guns and while bombs crashed through the hospital roof."

Through cold and heat, by days and dreary nights of ceaseless care, Nursing Sister Fortescue was ever brave and unafraid, knowing nothing else save the doing of her duty, no matter what the cost.

We who received her tender ministrations have the proud and reverent memory of "a good woman."

Nursing Sister Fortescue **was mentioned in Despatches** (London Gazette, 28 May, 1918) for gallant and distinguished services, and devotion to duty, at No. 3 Canadian Casualty Clearing Station.

NOTE: MID or Mentioned in dispatches meant that the person did **something above and beyond, or an act of bravery. It might have been a bar on a medal and als**o a citation.

Sister Fortescue was unmarried and drowned in the sinking of the Llandovery Castle on June 27th at the age of 40 with thirteen other valiant Nursing Sisters.

Margaret Jane Fortescue

She would have received the British
War Medal, Victory Medal and possibly others.

Nursing Sister Margaret Jane Fortescues' grave reference is found on

Panel 2 of the Halifax Memorial.

Matron Margaret Marjory Fraser
1885 - 1918

Nursing Sister and Matron Margaret (Pearl) Fraser was born in New Glasgow on March 20th., 1884, the third of Duncan Cameron and Elizabeth Fraser's five children. Margaret grew up between Guysborough, New Glasgow and Halifax. Margaret's father was a lawyer and from 1906 to 1910 was Lieutenant Governor of Nova Scotia. He passed away in 1910.

Margaret Marjorie "Pearl" Fraser
Born March 1884 Died: June 27th., 1918

Margaret completed her nursing training in 1909 at the Lady Stanley Institute for Trained Nurses in Ottawa. I understand Margaret also worked at the Vancouver General hospital in 1912.

When the war broke out in August 1914, Pearl Travelled to Quebec City and on September 28th. She enlisted with the Canadian Army Medical Corps.

Pearl was joined by her newly enlisted younger brother Alistair. They both travelled to Camp Valcartier with a Saskatchewan unit then were assigned to the 17th Battalion in Nova Scotia.

Pearl and Alistair both travelled across the North Atlantic to England with the First Canadian contingent in October 1914.

Pearl's first official assignment was with the No 1 Canadian General Hospital (CGH) and when she arrived in England was transferred to No 2 Canadian Stationary Hospital (CSH) on November 1st., 1914 and immediately was sent to France with the unit.

That unit was the first Canadian unit to set foot in France with the original staff qualifying for the **"Mons Star"** given to personnel serving in the war before December 31st., 1914.

In April or May, 1915 they received Canadian casualties from the second Battle of Ypres in which for the first time , poison gas was used as a warfare agent.

In October 1915 Pearl's unit relocated to Outreau, on the outskirts of Boulogne.

In 1916 Pearl was transferred to No 2 Casualty Clearing Station (CCS) and their 200 bed hospital at Aire-sur-la-Lys, close to Bethune, France. close enough to the front lines that the sounds of artillery fire was heard. While Pearl worked at No 2 CCS, she was also working with her 1st cousin Nursing sister Harriet Graham from New Glasgow.

From there, Pearl and the No 2 CCH unit relocated to Reme Siding, near Poprtingle, Belgium in mid November. An underground shelter was constructed for some protection from air raids.

In May 1917, Pearl returned to England and after about 30 months in France she was assigned to the Hospital ship HMHS Letitia used to transport wounded Canadian soldiers home.

Pearl made up to three crossings on this ship then on July 27th., 1917 was assigned to King's Red Cross Special Hospital, Bushey Park, England.

Pearl received her first promotion as "Nurse in Charge" of this 400 bed hospital which specialized in treating patients with heart and liver problems.

Pearl received a leave to visit her Graham relatives in New Glasgow, NS and also her mother Bessie in Moose jaw SK.

GEORGE
BORN MARCH 1, 1888
DIED JUNE 9, 1888

HARVEY GRAHAM
BORN OCT. 29, 1892
DIED AUG. 10, 1893

MARGARET MARGORY
BORN MARCH 21, 1884
LOST ON
H.M.S. LLANDOVERY CASTLE
JUNE 27, 1918

JAMES GIBSON LAURIER
BORN SEPT. 14, 1895
KILLED IN ACTION
MARCH 4, 1918

This memorial is at Riverside Cemetery, New Glasgow, Nova Scotia
Lot # 528 1/2

Returning to duty, Pearl was assigned to the HMHS ARAGuaya hospital ship which by war's end had completed 20 trans-Atlantic crossings having carried more than 15,000 wounded Canadian Soldiers home.

Pearl served on this ship during the winter of 1917-18.

Pearl was appointed Acting Matron of the 11,000 ton hospital ship Llandovery Castle in March 1918 and was aboard the ship when they landed 644 patients in Halifax.

Three days later, the Llandovery castle left for England with 97 CAMC staff and the Vessel's crew making the crossing.

The ship was chartered by the Canadian Government to carry sick and wounded from England to Halifax. The Llandovery Castle was Commanded by Capt. R.A. Sylvester a person consider to be an excellent seaman.

On the evening of June 27, 1918, the *Llandovery Castle* was approximately 190 kilometres west of Fastnet Rock, located near Ireland's southern tip, when a German U-boat spotted the vessel and sunk the ship.

Marjory's brother Alistair was severely wounded and a younger brother James Gibson Fraser had died in Action three months earlier.

Sister Marjory (Pearl) Fraser was unmarried. She drowned in the sinking of the Llandovery Castle on June 27th at the age of 33 with thirteen other Nursing Sisters.

She would have received the Mons Star, British War Medal and Victory Medal. (The "MONS STAR" was given to personnel serving in the war before December 31st., 1914).

Marjorie is also remembered on a family memorial in Riverside Cemetery (Lot 582-1/2) in New Glasgow as well as on a stained glass window of a local Presbyterian church in New Glasgow.

On the rear of the memoriam Marjorie's brother Alistair is remembered. He was was wounded twice while he was Aide decamp to General Curry.

Marjorie's younger brother who was killed in France in March 1918 is also remembered on this stone.

The Royal Canadian Legion in New Glasgow conducted a rededication ceremony at the cemetery and in the branch on June 27th., 2019. This was the 101'st anniversary of the sinking of the Llandovery Castle.

Pearl is the Nursing Sister on the right

Nursing Sister Marjory Pearl Frasers' grave reference is found on

Panel 1 of the Halifax Memorial.

Nursing Sister Minnie Katherine Gallaher
1880 - 1918

Nursing Sister Minnie Gallaher was born in Kingston, Ontario on January 1st., 1880. She was a daughter of Rev. John and Matilda Elder Gallaher of Pittsburg, Frontenac County, Ontario.

NURSING SISTER MINNIE GALLAHER Graduate of Protestant General Hospital. Drowned when Llandovery Castle was sunk in June, 1918.

Sister Minnie was a graduate of the Lady Stanley Institute in Ottawa, graduating in 1901. She became the assistant superintendent at the Protestant General Hospital, later taking a job as Superintendent at the Moosejaw, Sask. Hospital. Her siblings were: Ernest James Logan, Isabella Jane, John, Maude Elder, Joseph, Thomas Gillespie Smith, Mary, Margery Adams and Oscar Gesner.

She went overseas in the fall of 1915 with a number of other nurses from Ottawa. Minnie and Margaret Fraser were considered as close friends.

Sister Minnie Gallaher also had five uncles who served in WW1, three of them died.

Douglas, served with the First Australian Imperial Force (1 AIF, 11th Battalion) and was twice wounded at Gallipoli before being killed on June 3, 1916 at Laventie near Fromelles in France.

Dave Gallaher, a New Zealand rugby union footballer, died of wounds at Passchendaele, Belgium on October 4, 1917.

> Nursing Sister Minnie Katherine Gallagher, who is among the missing, was formerly asistant superintendent of the Ottawa General Hospital, from which training school she is a graduate. Her home is thought to have been Eganville. She was a close personal friend of Acting Matron Margaret Marjorie Fraser, whose name also appeared in the list, and who is a daughter of a former Lieutenant-Governor of Nova Scotia. Miss Gallagher is well known in Toronto, having been some years ago in charge of a model hospital camp at the Exhibition Grounds.
>
> Miss Gunn, superintendent of nurses at the Toronto General Hospital, declares that she is pretty sure most of the nurses on board the Llandovery Castle were from Ottawa, Montreal, Quebec and the Maritime Provinces. Very few of them were from Ontario, she thought.
>
> *Toronto Evening Telegram - July 5, 1918*

Henry, served with the Australian 51st Battalion and was killed on April 24, 1917.

Henry's twin brother, Charles, also served in the war and survived being badly wounded at Gallipoli. William, served with the Samoan Garrison from May 1918 to April 1920.

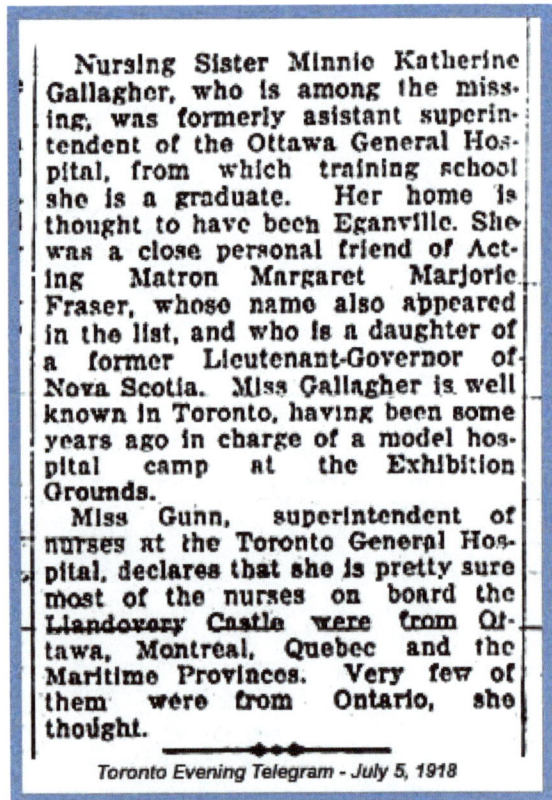

Nursing Sister Minnie Gallaher was unmarried. She drowned in the sinking of the Llandovery Castle on June 27th at the age of 33 with thirteen other Nursing Sisters.

Nursing Sister Gallaher Had not been back to Regent Street to visit her sisters and mother since her enlistment. Her big hope was when the ship docked at Halifax she would "take a run up to Ottawa to visit them".

Nursing sister Gallaher's parents, Rev. John and Matilda Elder Gallaher, like many parents, certainly gave up a lot for their country and freedom.

NURSING SISTER GALLAHER
Aboard Llandovery Castle
Was Born in Kingston
Was a Daughter of the Late Rev. John Gallaher, Pittsburg – a Queen's Doctor Also Abroad

The sinking of the Canadian hospital ship Llandovery Castle by a German U-boat, whereby a number of doctors, nurses and orderlies were drowned, has additional significance for Kingston. Beside Capt. the Rev D.G. MacPhail, it transpires that three others who formerly lived in Kingston were aboard that vessel. One was Nursing Sister Minnie Gallaher, daughter of the late Rev. John Gallaher of St. John's Presbyterian church, Pittsburg, who was born here thirty-nine years ago. Her mother, lives at 10 Regent Street, Ottawa. Mrs. Gallaher was a graduate of the Protestant General Hospital, Rideau Street, Ottawa. For some years before she went overseas, she was assisting superintendent of the Protestant General Hospital. She went overseas in the fall of 1915 with a number of other nurses from Ottawa.

The Kingston Whig-Standard, July 1, 1918

Gallaher's body was not recovered. This marker at her family plot in Beechwood Cemetery, Ottawa, reads:

"NURSING SISTER MINNIE K GALLAHER DROWNED IN SINKING OF HOSPITAL SHIP LLANDOVERY CASTLE JUNE 27TH, 1918. GREATER LOVE HATH NO MAN THAN THIS THAT A MAN LAY DOWN HIS LIFE FOR HIS FRIENDS."

Nursing Sister Minnie Gallaher's medals included British War medal, Victory medal) at least.

Nursing Sister Minnie Katherine Gallahers' grave reference is found on

Panel 2 of the Halifax Memorial.

Nursing Sister Jessie Mabel McDiarmid
1880 - 1918

Nursing Sister McDiarmid was born on August 14th., 1880 at Aston, Ontario.

She was the daughter of John McDiarmid of Beckwith Township, Ontario. She was also a neice of Mr. J. McDiarmid of Ashton, Ontario.

Nursing Sister Jessie Mabel McDiarmid was a professional nurse by trade, single, and served in an active militia.

Jessie was 5'5", dark complexion, dark eyes, brown hair, and Presbyterian.

She enlisted Sept 16, 1915 and was witnessed by Mary

Jessie M.Mc.Diarmid,Canadian Army Medical Corps drowned on the "Llandovery Castle" 27.6.18

Milligan. However, she had been working at the 5th General Hospital since July 30, 1915 as a civilian. She served as a nursing sister with the Canadian Army Medical Corps from Sept. 16, 1915 to June 27, 1918 when she died in the theatre of war.

She served on the Llandovery Castle, Hos pital Ship that contained the 5th General Hospital and was a merchant ship.

Jessie was stationed with the Medical Corps on Sept. 7, 1915 where she worked as the Matron in Chief. She enlisted on Sept. 16, 1915 in London and was assigned to the Red Cross Hospital in Taplow on Sept 27.

She was then sent to Salonica on Dec. 2, 1915 until Sept. 7, 1917. She was then posted to the No. 4 General Hospital on Sept. 29 in Basingstoke, England and then the No. 5 General Hospital in Liverpool. On Oct. 11.

It was noted she was mentioned in Dispatches on Nov. 28, 1917 likely due to when she left Salonika.

Being Mentioned In Dispatches MID is only done when a person does something far beyond the line of duty.

She was then posted to the Llandovery Castle on June 5, 1918 and drowned on her initial tour.

She was not declared officially dead until March 7, 1919 at the age of 37.

According to the Book of Remembrance, Jessie is listed on page 455 and served with the 5th General Hospital. Her family also received a dispatch on Oct. 17, 1917 from Lt.-Gen. GF Milne on behalf of the King thanking her for her service.

Her 1914-15 Star, Victory Medal and British War Medal were sent to her father, John McDiarmid but had it returned due to being unable to locate any next of kin.

Her pay was sent to the Royal Bank in Victoria, BC where she received $111 per month.

Jessie served as a nursing sister. While today we may think nurses have it easier than soldiers, it is clear they did not. Hospitals were not immune from bombing attacks and Nursing Sisters would have lived with that fear.

They also dealt with horrific injuries never seen before or during their training.

The earliest nursing sisters came from religious orders but by World War I, they tended to be professional nurses. They were called "Angels of Mercy" or bluebirds for their distinctive blue dresses, white aprons and white veils.

Nursing Sister Jessie McDiarmid was unmarried. She drowned in the sinking of the Llandovery Castle June 27th at the age 33 with thirteen other Nursing Sisters.

UNIT C. A. M. C.   Regimental No. _____

ATTESTATION PAPER.

CANADIAN OVER-SEAS EXPEDITIONARY FORCE.

QUESTIONS TO BE PUT BEFORE ATTESTATION.

1. What is your name? — Minnie Katherine Gallaher
2. In what Town, Township or Parish, and in what Country were you born? — Kingston. Canada.
3. What is the name of your next-of-kin? — Mrs M. C. Gallaher
4. What is the address of your next-of-kin? — 10 Regent St. Ottawa, Canada
5. What is the date of your birth? — June, 1880.
6. What is your Trade or Calling? — Nurse — Graduate
7. Are you married? — no
8. Are you willing to be vaccinated or re-vaccinated? — Yes.
9. Do you now belong to the Active Militia? — no
10. Have you ever served in any Military Force? — no
11. Do you understand the nature and terms of your engagement? — Yes.
12. Are you willing to be attested to serve in the Canadian Over-Seas Expeditionary Force? — Yes

Minnie K. Gallaher (Signature of Man.)
B. Henriette Casa... (Signature of Witness.)

DECLARATION TO BE MADE BY MAN ON ATTESTATION.

I Minnie K. Gallaher ... do solemnly declare that the above answers made by me to the above questions are true, and that I am willing to fulfil the engagements by me now made, and I hereby engage and agree to serve in the Canadian Over-Seas Expeditionary Force, and to be attached to any arm of the service therein, for the term of one year, or during the war now existing between Great Britain and Germany should that war last longer than one year, and for six months after the termination of that war provided His Majesty should so long require my services, or until legally discharged.

Minnie K. Gallaher (Signature of Recruit).
Date Sept. 2nd 1915. B. Henriette Casa... (Signature of Witness).

OATH TO BE TAKEN BY MAN ON ATTESTATION.

I, Minnie K. Gallaher ... do make Oath, that I will be faithful and bear true Allegiance to His Majesty King George the Fifth, His Heirs and Successors, and that I will as in duty bound honestly and faithfully defend His Majesty, His Heirs and Successors, in Person, Crown and Dignity, against all enemies, and will observe and obey all orders of His Majesty, His Heirs and Successors, and of all the Generals and Officers set over me. So help me God.

Minnie K. Gallaher (Signature of Recruit).
Date Sept. 2nd 1915. B. Henriette Casa... (Signature of Witness).

CERTIFICATE OF MAGISTRATE.

The Recruit above-named was cautioned by me that if he made any false answer to any of the above questions he would be liable to be punished as provided in the Army Act.

The above questions were then read to the Recruit in my presence.

I have taken care that he understands each question, and that his answer to each question has been duly entered as replied to, and the said Recruit has made and signed the declaration and taken the oath before me, at _____ this ____ day of _____ 1915.

Lawrence ... (Signature of Justice).

I certify that the above is a true copy of the Attestation of the above-named Recruit.

DL Clark (Approving Officer).

Some family member, on her behalf, would have received the Mons Star, British War Medal and Victory Medal at least.

Nursing Sister Jessie Mabel McDiarmids' grave reference is found on

Panel 2 of the Halifax Memorial.

Nursing Sister Mary Agnes McKenzie 1880 - 1918

Nursing Sister McKenzie was born on April 28th., 1880 and raised in Toronto, Ontario.

Her parents were Mary and Thomas McKenzie, both Scottish immigrants to Canada.

She went to school in St. Jamestown as a young girl — at the Rose Avenue School, which is still there today. Her friends called her Nan.

Nursing Sister McKenzie had a sister Christina and two brothers, Donald and Walter. She graduated from the Rochester General Hospital in 1903.

Nursing Sister McKenzie was still just a teenager when she decided she wanted to become a nurse. She got a job at a hospital in Toronto and, in the years before the war broke out, got some experience working at the Military Hospital in Halifax. She was Presbyterian and at her enlistment date was living at 290 McPherson Avenue in Toronto.

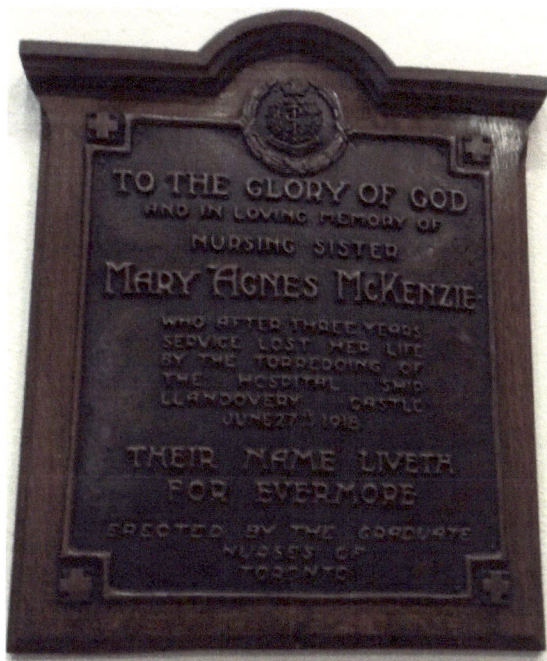

Nursing Sister McKenzie served with the Canadian Army Medical Corps as a military nurse from 1911 and enlisted in the CAMC on January 31st., 1916.

Her first posting was to the Ontario Military Hospital at Orpington, Kent.

Sister McKenzie, wanting a trip home for a visit while she served on the Llandovery Castle hospital ship.

While the ship had been docked in Halifax, she'd hoped for a chance to come home to Toronto for a brief visit with her family. But all leave had been cancelled.

She promised her mom she would try again the next time they were back in Canada.

Sister McKenzie is still remembered — along with a few other nurses from the Ontario Military Hospital who died in

WWI — with a plaque inside Queen's Park. And she's also remembered in a memorial at her grade school, Rose Avenue School.

Nursing Sister McKenzie was unmarried. She drowned in the sinking of the Llandovery Castle on June 27th at the age of 38 with thirteen other Nursing Sisters.

Unit *Ontario Military Hosp* Rank *N. S.* Name *McKenzie, Mary Agnes*

OFFICERS' DECLARATION PAPER

CANADIAN OVER-SEAS EXPEDITIONARY FORCE

QUESTIONS TO BE ANSWERED BY OFFICER

(ANSWERS)

1. (a) What is your Surname? *McKenzie*

   (b) What are your Christian Names? *Mary Agnes*

2. (a) Where were you born? (State place and country) *Toronto, Ont.*

   (b) What is your present address? *290 McPherson Ave. Toronto Ont.*

3. What is the date of your birth? *Apr. 28th /80.*

4. What is (a) the name of your next-of-kin? *Thomas C. McKenzie*

   (b) the address of your next-of-kin? *290 McPherson Ave. Toronto, Ont.*

   (c) the relationship of your next-of-kin? *father*

5. What is your profession or occupation? *Nurse*

6. What is your religion? *Presbyterian*

7. Are you willing to be vaccinated or re-vaccinated and inoculated? *yes*

8. To what Unit of the Active Militia do you belong? *C. A. M. C.*

9. State particulars of any former Military Service. *N. S., C. A. M. C. 1911.*

10. Are you willing to serve in the

    CANADIAN OVER-SEAS EXPEDITIONARY FORCE? *yes*

The undersigned hereby declares that the above answers made by him to the above questions are true.

Mary A. McKenzie (Signature of Officer.)

CERTIFICATE OF MEDICAL EXAMINATION

I have examined the above-named Officer in accordance with the Regulations for Army Medical Services.

I consider ~~him~~* *her* ... *fit* ... for the CANADIAN OVER-SEAS EXPEDITIONARY FORCE.

Date *January 31st* 191 6.

Place *Toronto, Ont.*

Medical Officer.

*Insert here "fit" or "unfit"

M. F. W. 51

She would have received the British War Medal and Victory Medal at least.

Nursing Sister Mary Agnes McKenzies' grave reference is found on

Panel 2 of the Halifax Memorial.

Nursing Sister Rena McLean
1879 - 1918

Nursing Sister Rena Maude McLean was born on June 14th., 1879 in Souris, P.E.I. to John McLean and Matilda Jane Jury. John McLean was a successful businessman and Conservative politician.

Nursing Sister Rena McLean studied at Mount Allison ladies' college in Sackville in 1891 and 1892. She attended the Halifax Ladies College, graduating in 1896.

She then studied nursing at the Newport Hospital in Newport, Rhode Island, USA. She completed her nurses training in 1908.

Sister McLean was appointed head nurse in

Rena McLean

the operating room at the Henry Heywood Memorial Hospital in Gardner, Mass.

After this she enlisted for service and was appointed to the Canadian Army Medical Corps on September 28th., 1914.

Nursing Sister McLean left for Britain and was sent to France with the No. 2 Canadian Stationary Hospital.

In Le Touquet (Le Touquet-Paris-Plage) she was one of 35 Canadian nurses who helped convert a luxurious hotel into the first hospital in France that was completely staffed by Canadians.

There, in the spring of 1915, 1,100 Canadian soldiers, victims of chlorine gas at the second battle of Ypres, passed through the wards on their way back to Britain.

Nursing Sisters and Matron Strong of the No. 2 Stationary Hospital in France, ca 1916.
(Library and Archives Canada Photo, MIKAN No. 3604213)

Nursing Sister McLean would have worked with Nursing sisters, Harriet Graham and Marjorie (Pearl) Fraser at this hospital as I have a letter from Nursing sister Harriet Graham explaining how they converted the large residence and tried to get the largest ward called the "Nova Scotia Ward".

Later that year Nursing Sister McLean served briefly with No.12 British Stationary Hospital at Rouen and then joined the Duchess of Connaught's Canadian Red Cross Hospital in Taplow, England.

After a return to Canada on transport duty, she proceeded to Salonica (Thessaloniki), Greece, in October 1916 for service with No.1 Canadian Stationary Hospital. There was controversy in Britain over nurses having been sent to the Mediterranean and all were returned the next year.

McLean then joined No.16 Canadian General Hospital in Orpington (London).

Nursing Sister Rena McLean had been an attractive, fun-loving woman, consider kind and caring. As her last letter, written on board the LLANDOVERY CASTLE on 16 June, illustrates, she had kept her morale high in spite of the years spent in some of the worst areas of the war.

"Here we are once more approaching Halifax, but still as far from home as ever. . . . This trip more than half our patients are amputation cases and would make you heartsick only they are so cheerful and happy themselves. . . . This may be my last trip over and, if it is, that means that I don't get home until dear knows when, for as soon as I get to England I am going to put in for France and once there it will be hard enough to get away."

Nursing Sister McLean had a brief postings to the hospital ship ARAGUAYA and again to No.16 General Hospital. She was assigned in March 1918 to the *Llandovery* CASTLE, which carried Canadian wounded to Halifax.

She died on the voyage back to England when the vessel was torpedoed and sunk by the enemy off the coast of Ireland on 27 June 1918. All 14 nursing sisters on board perished.

Plaques in memory of Rena McLean are located in St James United Church in Souris, in Mount Allison's Memorial Library, and in the X-ray laboratory at Queen Elizabeth Hospital in Charlottetown. A 200-bed hospital for veterans in Charlottetown was named after her in 1919 but was closed within a year or so.

In Canada, the Canadian Forces Medical Services School at Canadian Forces Base Borden, Ont., gives the Llandovery Castle Award each year to the most deserving nursing officer.

Rena Maude McLean's medals are held by the Borden Memorial Museum and Arch. at Canadian Forces Base Borden, Ont. They were placed there by Dr Gustave Gingras following the death of his wife, Rena M. MacLean Gingras.

She would have received the Mons Star, British War Medal and Victory Medal at least.

Nursing Sister Rena McLeans' grave reference is found on

Panel 2 of the Halifax Memorial.

Nursing Sister Gladys Irene Sare
1889 - 1918

Nursing Sister Sare was born on June 6th., 1889 in Bath, Somerset, England. Her mother was Annie Garlick (Shackell) Sare (1858-1941) of west Hill avenue, Notre-dame de Grace, Montreal, Quebec.

Her father was Henry Frank Sare.

Nursing Sister Sare had a brother; Major Harry Frank Sare (1879-1917) and Robert George Sare (1881-1965) he married in 1912.

She also had a sister; Muriel Annie Sare born in 1895. Nursing Sister Sares' brother Major Harry Frank Sare , 'D' Company, 87th Batallion was killed in action in April, 1917.

He is buried at Villers Station Cemetery, Villers-au-Bois.

His son, Lieutenant Lionel Sare, went on to serve during the Korean war.

Nursing Sister Sare graduated from the Montreal General Hospital with the class of 1913.

A plaque I remembrance of Nursing Sister Sare hangs in the main Corridor (near Livingstone Hall) Montreal General Hospital. It says:

Nursing Sister Sare enlisted on 26th January 1916 at General Hospital Laval.

She was transferred to the CAMC on 22nd February 1917.

Her next transfer was to No. 6. Canadian General Hospital on 5th March 1917. She then was posted to H.M.H.S. Letitia on 19th June 1917 and from there she served at other Canadian general hospitals in England.

She was posted to H.M.H.S. Llandovery Castle on 7th June 1918. On 27th June 1918 at 9:30pm Hospital Ship Llandovery Castle was torpedoed and Nursing sister Gladys Irene Sare drowned, as did the other 13 sisters.

I have been unable to find a picture of Nursing Sister Sare.

"This tablet has been erected by the members of the Montreal General Hospital Alumnae Association in memory of Nursing Sisters Margaret Jane Fortescue and Gladys Irene Sare, who were drowned when H.M. hospital ship 'Llandovery Castle' was torpedoed by a German submarine, June 27th, 1918."

She would have received the British War Medal and Victory Medal at least.

No picture is available.

Nursing Sister Glady Irene Sares' grave reference is found on

Panel 2 of the Halifax Memorial.

Nursing Sister Anna Irene Stamers
1888 - 1918

Nursing sister Stamers was born on January 15th., 1888 in Saint John, New Brunswick. Her mother was Mrs. S. Lavinia Stamers of 171 Waterloo St., Saint John, NB.

Sister Stamers was described as slender, about 5' 7 inches, brown hair and blue eyes.

Nursing Sister Stamers enlisted in the CAMC on June 3rd., 1915.

Nursing Sister Anna Marie Stamers

Her first assignment was to #1 Canadian General Hospital in Etaples, France. The hospital was close to a training base and the railway and a easy bombing target. It and other hospiotals were eventually bombed.

Four months later she, herself became a patient at the #24 General Hospital with an infection. From there she was transferred to a convelescent home in Paris Plage.

Having fully recovered she returned to duty.

#21 Casualty Clearing Station

IN GRATEFUL MEMORY OF
NURSING SISTER
ANNA IRENE STAMERS
C·A·M·C·
LOST AT SEA ON
S·S·LLANDOVERY CASTLE
TORPEDOED 27TH JUNE 1918

ERECTED BY SAINT JOHN
MUNICIPAL CHAPTER I·O·D·E·

In January, 1917 Nursing Sister Stamers was given two weeks leave and in May 1917 she was transferred back to England and posted to the Hospital Ship in Orpington, Kent.

In March 1918, she was transferred to the Llandovery castle After several journeys to Canada caring for the wounded passangers she was given a short leave.

In July Nursing sister Stamers boarded the Llandover Castle for the return journey to Canada. The ship was torpoded and she and her 13 other nursing friends were all drowned.

Canadian Army Medical Corps medical staff in rubble of bombed hospital in France

The memorial stone shown in her memory, can be found in the veteran's section of the Fernhill Cemetery in Saint John, New Brunswick, where she was born.

She would have received the British War Medal and Victory Medal at least.

Nursing Sister Anna Irene Stamers' grave reference is found on

Panel 2 of the Halifax Memorial

Nursing Sister Jean Templeman
1885 - 1918

Nursing Sister Jean Templeman was born on June 18th., 1885 at Montreal, Quebec. Her father was J. Templeman of 218 Strathcona Avenue in Ottawa. She attended school at the Ottawa Collegiate Institute.

Nursing Sister Templeman enlisted on June 3rd., 1915 at Montreal, Canada with the Canadian Expeditionary Force as a Nursing Sister. She was 30 years of age, five ft tall, 105 pounds with grey eyes and brown hair.

Nursing Sister Templeman's first posting was #1 Canadian General Hospital. From February 22nd. until July she served at the #21 Casualty Clearing Station, from there, on May 28th., 1917 she was posted to the Ontario Military Hospital at Orpington, Kent, serving there until June 4th., 1918.

Ambulances, carrying four patients brought in the wounded to the clearing stations. A group closer to the front line did an initial assessment doing some immediate treatment before transporting them to the hospital.

Nursing Sister Templeman was stationed there from May 2017 until she was posted to the Hospital ship Llandovery Castle in June 1918. On the return journey to Canada. The ship was torpoded and she and her 13 other nursing friends were all drowned.

Nursing Sister Templeman is remembered on a memorial at the Ottawa Collegiate Institure. It says:

"To the memory of Ex-Pupils of the Ottawa Collegiate Institute who in defence of justice and freedom generously gave their lives in the great war".

Nursing Sister Templeman wrote to her father; "I am on transport duty and probably will be all summer, perhaps till Christmas." She had been home on leave the previous summer, and her father was making travel plans to see her the next time the ship called at a Canadian port. But the nurses never came home again.

She would have received the British War Medal and Victory Medal at least. Records show that the medals went to her father.

Nursing Sister Jean Templeman's grave reference is found on

Panel 2 of the Halifax Memorial.

CHAPTER 12

LETTER HOME FROM A RED CROSS NURSE

This letter gives an indication of the duties of a war nursing sister at the time:

From Red Cross Nurse. - Miss Harriet Graham - December, 1914

Canada No. 2 Stationary Hospital, France

Dear---------------

I'm sorry not to have gotten a letter off to you before this, but we have been on the jump and have been awfully busy, and now I have all beds turned down and am waiting for the ambulances to come in with their loads.

NAME.	RANK.	NUMBER.	UNIT.	HONOUR OR AWARD.
GRAHAM Miss. Harriet.	Nursing Sister.		Canadian A.M.C. Canadian Nursing Service	Royal Red Cross. 2nd Class.

AUTHORITY.	DATE.	DETAILS. TO BE CONTINUED ON BACK OF CARD IF NECESSARY.	MENTIONED IN DESPATCHES. AUTHORITY.	DATE.
L.G. 30111	4-6-17.			

OTHER AWARDS.		
NATURE.	AUTHORITY.	DATE.

It is great, and we love it. We have a dandy crowd of girls and a very nice crowd of officers, and our men are as willing as can be, though most of them are untrained: but when I see the poor souls scrubbing and doing all sorts of things they never did before, I can't but feel sorry for them. But I must start at the beginning of my story.

We have the most beautiful hospital you could imagine, and we are simply proud of ourselves, for the FIRST Canadian Hospital to be in France.

We just came here and commandeered a beautiful summer hotel, turned into it, and settled ourselves. Then we took a house belonging to Count Constaudivitch, who married Miss Cutting of New York, and who is in Servia or someplace on war business, for the nurses to live in, and another for the officers.

They are all right together, so it makes it quite nice, and a comfortable bed to turn into at night when we get off duty. But our hospital is grand. There were big verandas on three sides, which have been enclosed in glass, and make fine wards.

I tell you, if you think house cleaning is hard work, and you know I do think it, I hope I don't have to clean another hotel; but we had some fun out of it too. Col. Shilling said he was going to name all the wards for the different provinces. So I said: "Well please put Nova Scotia in the dining room." The dining room , I must explain, is the biggest ward and right at the main entrance.

"that's it 'J he said, "Sister Graham always wants Nova Scotia to have the biggest and best place right in front; that is the place for Ontario, as most of the corps come from there." One of the other girls said: "But British Columbia is the biggest province." "Well," I said, "We will all have to put the names in a hat and draw for it," and the fun of it is Nova Scotia has it – the prettiest ward, with seventy-five beds and the most important place. We are all extremely pleased.

I'm going to send to Dr. Neily and see if he can get a Nova Scotia flag for it. At present I am sitting in Quebec, as they are going to receive tonight.

Pearl Fraser is on night duty, but it is not so awful, or at least has not been so far, as the nights we receive we all stay in and help. You know, they always come in at night.

We have fifteen ambulances and they each carry four patients, and when they all make about three trips, it makes quite a number of patients.

I'm not allowed to tell you how many patients we have or how many we can take, but you can tell Kit we can take twice as many as St. Luke's, and, of course, may have to take more than that at any time. Oh! My, but it is great.

I just love it, even though it's ten o'clock now and I have been on the go all day, and they have not started to come in yet.

I see where we don't get to bed tonight.

By the time we get the poor souls into bed and half way clean and a dressing done, its morning before you know it, and the poor creatures, you would be sorry for them, they are so filthy, and many times just alive with vermin.

Pearl said tonight: "isn't it funny, in our hospital we despised men who were dirty, and here the worse they are, the better we like them." When they say, "keep away sister, I'm so dirty, but I have been in the trenches, and I haven't had a bath for so many weeks," I just feel like saying, "I honor your dirt-!"

I hear we are getting a consignment of Germans tonight. I wonder sometimes if it is a sin to feel so awful for our enemies. I don't know if there is much in the papers at home about, them and the awful things they do.

4 a.m. - The ambulances started to come just then, so I had to stop, and now must turn in, as 7 a.m comes soon, and I will try to finish this tomorrow.

Dec. 4. – It is time again to go to bed, I suppose, but it seems to be the only time for letter writing, and I know how you all at home must look for a line, and then it seems so far to send a letter with nothing in it. When we get our hospital in better running order, we may have more time; though, of course, we are all dreading the spring and the diseases that must come in this war.

Our patients of last night are mostly happy today. I spend all the spare pennies I can find on cigarettes for them, poor boys, it seems to do more to quiet their nerves than anything else. I wish I could tell you some of their tales, but I'm afraid my letter would never go by the censor.

One of my patients is just a lad of eighteen, and the nicest kind of a kid. He told me his two pals were shot and killed. I said: "Weren't you awfully afraid?" "Yes sister," he said, "I was awfully afraid at first; there was just thirty yards between the German trenches and ours; but I soon got over it.

You see sister, it's like this, there is no use trying to dodge them, if the bullet's for you, you'll get it." He then asked me if it would be long before he could go back. "Why", I said, "do you want to go back?" He just looked at me and said: "Does anybody want to go to Hell, sister?" and, poor kid, he will have to go back, because he is not very badly injured.

Some of the tales they tell are awful, too terrible to write about. The "Jack Johnsons," as the Tommies call the German's big guns, are really devilish, and although we are as far from the firing as three-quarters of the way to Truro, still the guns can be heard quite distinctly at night. That will give you some idea what the noise must be close up, and is it any wonder that the poor boys' nerves are in most cases completely gone, - but I must not write of such things.

Miss McDonald was here to see us, and we were so glad to have her. She is so nice, and I get fonder of her all the time. If we are here, and if she can manage it, and a few more "if's" she is coming to spend Christmas with us. I suppose it will be nearly Christmas before you get this, possibly after. Give my love and best wishes to all the friends.

I received some Halifax papers last night from Mr. Neilly, one of which gave a list of the Pictou County boys going in the next contingent. I was sorry not to see more familiar names from New Glasgow. I am afraid they don't realize what this war means. I tell you it's awful to think of when our boys come over, but I would be ashamed if Wendell was any place but right where he is now.

Well, I must stop and turn in.

HARRIET

NOTES: The First Canadian Hospital (CSH) referred to in the letter, was the first unit to set foot in France with the original staff qualifying for the "Mons Star" given to people serving in the war before Dec 31st., 1914.

This letter was written in 1914, to her parents, Harvey and Hannah Graham

Harriet Graham, (the writer of this letter) Daughter of Harvey Graham, 1848-1907 was born in 1883 in New Glasgow and died in 1932. * buried at Riverside Cemetery.

Wendell Stewart Graham, Harriet's brother born 1879, also served in the first war and died in 1945. * Buried at Riverside Cemetery.

Marjorie (Pearl) Fraser was the daughter of D.C. and Bessie Fraser and a 1st cousin to Wendell and Harriet. Marjorie was born in 1884 and died in 1918 when the Hospital Ship Llandovery Castle Hospital ship was torpedoed. Marjorie is remembered on a Monument with her brother Laurie Fraser in Riverside Cemetery in New Glasgow, who died in the trench in France 3 months after his sister Marjorie.

NOTE:

Despite the fact that the Canadian hospital was distinguished by red crosses and not located near military installations, it was still attacked. The air raid occurred on May 29, 1918, shortly after midnight. Although the attack was done by a single German aircraft, it still left 32 staff and patients dead and 17 wounded.

It is interesting to note that Canadian nurses where the only nurses within the Allied armies who held the rank of officers. This rank is why Canadian officers were adamant that heroic Canadian nurses were commemorated for their valour. There was a **strong push back from British officials** who initially refused to award Canadian nurses any honours because they were women. In regards to the general public, although no one was really surprised that women would be sympathetic towards the war effort, the fact that they contributed in such a physical manner was baffling. Nothing pissed off the public like a nurse getting killed so the nursing sisters wound up being propaganda fodder.

The first Canadian Hospital was eventually bombed in 1918. The air raid occurred on May 29, 1918, shortly after midnight. Although the attack was done by a single German aircraft, it still left 32 staff and patients dead and 17 wounded.

CHAPTER 13

BATHHOUSES AT THE FRONT

Not all the women were nurses. Many served in other capacities. The system of bathhouses established for keeping the men clean was rather elaborate. Every three weeks the troops underwent a thorough cleaning. Reaching bathhouses their uniforms were sterilized and they were provided with fresh underwear. By this method vermin generally regarded as dreaded germ carriers were eliminated.

Some 16 thousand women were engaged at the bathing stations in sterilizing uniforms. There was a general absence of malarial diseases on the Western front. The few cases discovered from time to time were confined for the most part to soldiers from the southern climates. Trench fever was more prevalent than other diseases.

There were times when 100,000 men suffering from trench fever were confined to hospitals.

CHAPTER 14

THE MURDER OF NURSING SISTER EDITH CAVELL

Huntingdon Gleaner, Huntingdon, Quebec - Thursday, October 28, 1915

Nursing Sister Edith Cavell had long been suspected by the Germans as being a spy, but she always refused to leave so long as there was a single wounded man left in Brussels, saying that duty compelled her to remain where there was suffering. It is believed that before her arrest she was spied upon.

Little is known of the trial, but it is reported that when the President of the court asked if she wished to add anything to her defense or to sign a request for the German Emperor's pardon she merely shrugged her shoulders and walked out.

She was as brave before the German rifles as she had been before the court-martial, and refused to have her eyes bandaged. She pinned a small Union Jack on her dress.

The Rev. Mr. Graham, an Anglican clergyman at Brussels, was allowed to see Miss Cavell before she was shot. The following is Mr. Graham's account of the interview:

On Monday evening, Oct. 11th, I was admitted by a special passport from the German authorities to the prison of St. Giles, where Miss Edith Cavell had been confined for ten weeks. The final sentence had been given early that afternoon.

To my astonishment and relief, I found my friend perfectly calm and resigned, but this could not lessen the tenderness and intensity of feeling on either part during that last interview of almost an hour.

Her first words to me were upon a matter concerning herself personally, but the solemn asseveration which accompanied them was made expressly in the light of God and eternity. She then added that she wished all her friends to know that she willingly gave her life for her country, and said: "I have no fear were shrinking, I have seen death so often that it is not strange or fearful to me."

She further said: "I thank God for this ten weeks of quiet before the end. My life has always been hurried and full of difficulties; this time the rest has been a great mercy. They have all been very kind to me here. But this I would say: standing as they do in view of God and eternity I realize that patriotism is not enough. I must have no hatred or bitterness towards anyone."

We partook of the Holy Communion together, and she received the Gospel message of consolation with all her heart. At the close of the little service I began to repeat the words "Abide with me" and she joined softly to the end.

We sat quietly talking until it was time for me to go. She gave me parting messages to relatives and friends. She spoke of her soul's needs at the moment, and she received the assurance of God's words as only a Christian can do.

Then I said goodbye, and she smiled and said, "We shall meet again."

ABOUT THE AUTHOR

William Graham was born in Sydney, Nova Scotia in 1940 and continued
his life in Ontario in 1985. He is a husband to Shirley, a father,
grandfather and great grandfather who has had an
interesting life doing many different things.
As he get older the things that become
increasingly important in his life are;
religion, family and groups he
and Shirley can support to
help those in need.

www.ingramcontent.com/pod-product-compliance
Lightning Source LLC
Chambersburg PA
CBHW041531090426
42738CB00036B/110